GABRIELLE

REECE

GABRIELLE REECE

VOLLEYBALL'S MODEL ATHLETE

Terri Morgan

Lerner Publications Company ● Minneapolis

This book is available in two editions:
Library binding by Lerner Publications Company
Soft cover by First Avenue Editions
241 First Avenue North
Minneapolis, Minnesota 55401

Website address: www.lernerbooks.com

Library of Congress Cataloging-in-Publication Data

Morgan, Terri.
    Gabrielle Reece, volleyball's model athlete / Terri Morgan.
        p.   cm.
    Includes bibliographical references and index.
    Summary: Examines the life and achievements of the award-winning
professional beach volleyball player who is also a fashion model and
television personality.
    ISBN 0–8225–3667–6 (alk. paper)
    ISBN 0–8225–9828–0 (pbk. : alk. paper)
    1. Reece, Gabrielle—Juvenile literature. 2. Volleyball players—
United States—Biography—Juvenile literature. [1. Reece,
Gabrielle. 2. Volleyball players. 3. Women—Biography.]
I. Title. II. Title: Gabrielle Reece.
GV1015.26.R44M67   1999
796.325'092—dc21
    [B]   98–32265

Manufactured in the United States of America
1 2 3 4 5 6 – JR – 04 03 02 01 00 99

Contents

Gabrielle Reece is a force on the beach.

1

Queen of the Beach

The nudging and whispering starts as soon as Gabrielle Reece begins walking on the sands of Main Beach in Santa Cruz, California. *Look,* spectators murmur, gently elbowing their friends to get their attention. *It's her!*

For fans of the women's professional four-on-four beach volleyball tour, no other explanation is needed. Heads swivel, and necks crane. Within seconds, nearly every eye on the beach is focused on a slender 6-foot, 3-inch woman in navy blue sweatpants and a loose-fitting Nike T-shirt. Gabrielle is making her way to the competitors' tent. By the time Gabby, as she's known to her fans, reaches her destination, the entire beach is buzzing. More than a thousand spectators have gathered on the beach to watch the early rounds of the tournament. It seems as though every one of the fans is saying *Gabby's here,* at the same time.

Gabby focuses on her opponents.

Even with her features hidden beneath a visor and behind wraparound sunglasses, the 170-pound former supermodel is instantly recognized. After having been on the cover of dozens of fashion magazines, having been named as one of *People* magazine's 50 Most Beautiful People, and having hosted her own sports show on MTV, Gabby is used to being noticed. But on this foggy, late summer morning, Gabby isn't thinking about her reputation as a cover girl. Instead, she's preparing to lead Team Nike on the sand court of the 4-on-4 Pro Beach Volleyball League tournament this afternoon.

Gabby's modeling career has earned her fame and fortune. Many fans wonder why she even plays professional sports. For Gabby, the answer to that question—which she hears everywhere she goes—is simple. Modeling and television work are just jobs. Volleyball is her real love.

"I understand that, yeah, I could probably walk away and just do TV," Gabby said. "From the business side, that is probably a good idea." But walking away from her favorite sport is not an option for Gabby.

"Volleyball is my foundation for everything," Gabby says. "I have a lot of respect for the role it plays, and there's a certain amount of credibility that comes with it."

Inside the players' tent, Gabby reaches into her beach bag for a water bottle as her teammates gather around. Bending forward slightly at the waist, and lowering her voice so her competitors can't overhear, Gabby, Jennifer Meredith, Christine Romero, and Chrissy Boehle begin talking about strategy. Miscommunication in their previous round against the Paul Mitchell team cost them a victory. Gabby wants to make sure the mistake isn't repeated.

The sun breaks through the fog by the time Team Nike and Team Discus meet for the fifth round of the **round-robin tournament.** What had been a cold, gloomy day has become a warm and bright one. On the court, another change has taken place. Gabby's prematch smile has been replaced with a grimace. Her hair has been drawn back into a ponytail. She's wearing lycra shorts instead of sweatpants. Gabby's T-shirt is off to reveal a fitness top. Gabby is ready for action.

As a **middle blocker,** Gabby takes a position in front of the net at the center as the match begins.

Gabby is the captain and middle blocker for Team Nike.

With knees slightly bent and legs relaxed, she lunges to her left, stretching her long, muscular arms above the net. The volleyball streaks toward her. With a quick flick of her wrists that puts her strong hands into position to stop the ball, Gabby blocks the shot. The ball drops on Team Discus's side of the net.

Moments later, Gabby crouches low as Jennifer Johnson, Team Discus's rookie **outside hitter,** hits the ball. As the ball reaches its peak, Gabby straightens her legs and jumps. Her feet are about eight inches off the ground when she swings her powerful right arm up from its position behind her back. Her motion is so quick that her arm blurs like the spokes of a bicycle wheel speeding down a steep hill. Spectators first hear, then see, Gabby's right palm smack the ball. Grunting as she makes contact, Gabby spikes the volleyball over the net and onto the sand. The league's Offensive Player of the Year in 1994 and 1995 has just tallied her first **kill** shot of the match. Team Discus's **setter** Stephanie Cox, who dives for the ball in an attempt to save it, hits the sand a split second after the volleyball does.

The crowd roars its approval. By the end of the tournament, Gabby has tallied 51 kills in four matches. That raises her kill total for the 12-tournament season to 547. That's the most kills recorded in the league's six-year history. Kim Oden finishes second on the kill list for 1996, with 439.

Nike scores the first three points before Team Discus gets on the board. Another loud, spectacular spike by Gabby increases Nike's lead back to three points. Moments later, Nike is up by five points, then six, before Team Discus rallies briefly to stay in the match. Finally, with Nike leading 14–8, Gabby spikes the ball into the front left corner of the opposite court to close out the match.

Following the victory, Gabby stops frequently on her way back to the competitors' tent. She signs autographs, chats with her fans, and answers reporters' questions. Not surprisingly, many questions center around her careers. Gabby, who has heard all the questions dozens of times, answers them patiently and politely. "I think people are surprised that they can look at Gabby on television or in a magazine and say she's competitive and even in some ways a dominant force playing volleyball," she says.

Bouncing Around

2

Gabrielle Reece was born in La Jolla, California, on January 6, 1970. Her father, Robert Eduardo Reece, had been born and raised on a small island in the Caribbean Sea known as Trinidad. Located off the northeast coast of Venezuela, the tropical island is part of a large group of islands known as the West Indies. Along with neighboring Tobago, Trinidad is a former British Colony. In 1962, the two islands became an independent country known as Trinidad and Tobago.

Gabby's mother, Terry Glynn, had grown up on Long Island, New York. Gabby's parents met in San Diego, California, in 1969. At that time, Gabby's father was studying for his master's degree in human behavior at the United States International University.

The two quickly liked each another. For one thing, they both shared an obvious trait. Bobby, as Robert's friends called him, was just over 6 feet tall. Terry, at 6 feet, 2 inches, was even taller. Gabby, the couple's only child, got her height from both parents and her striking green eyes from her father.

Gabby's parents separated when she was two. Following the breakup, Gabby moved to Mexico City with her mother. Terry found a job training dolphins for a circus. After living in Mexico for about a year, Gabby developed a bad cough. Doctors diagnosed her ailment as whooping cough, a serious respiratory infection. Terry decided that Mexico City's polluted air wasn't healthy for her young daughter. So she sent Gabby to Long Island, New York, to live with Terry's best friends, Norette and Joe Zucarello.

Gabby spent her early childhood in New York.

Aunt Norette and Uncle Joe, as Gabby calls them, were delighted. They were childless and welcomed the three-year-old into their home. Treating Gabby as if she were their own daughter, the Zucarellos often took her on outings, and signed her up for many different activities. Some, like swimming lessons, Gabby enjoyed. Others, like ballet classes, she hated. Shortly after Gabby arrived, the Zucarellos got a white Samoyed dog. "We gave her security when she needed it, but she gave us much more," Norette says. "She was our child."

Every so often, Gabby's dad would come to Long Island to visit Gabby. Those visits stopped when Gabby was five. Bobby Reece died in a plane crash. He had been wearing a silver cross on a necklace when he was killed. It was given to his daughter after his death, and the necklace remains one of Gabby's most cherished possessions.

One day, when Gabby was seven, Gabby's mother called the Zucarellos. Terry had remarried. She and her husband, an attorney named Jose Beauchamp, were living in Puerto Rico. Puerto Rico is an American territory in the Atlantic Ocean southeast of Florida. Terry wanted Gabby to come and live there with her and her new husband.

Gabby, already 5 feet tall, didn't want to leave the Zucarellos. "I stood on the sofa in their house on Long Island, crying, 'Can't you get a lawyer?'" Gabby wrote in her book, *Big Girl in the Middle.*

The Zucarellos didn't want Gabby to leave either, but they respected Terry's wishes. Norette says she cried every day for the next 12 months because she missed Gabby so much.

Shortly after being reunited with her mother, Gabby and her family moved to St. Thomas, in the Virgin Islands. Located just east of Puerto Rico, St. Thomas is also a territory of the United States. The family settled into a house located in a ravine on the north shore of St. Thomas. Gabby would often play in the ravine with her two dogs, Lady and Felisse.

Terry and Gabby in St. Thomas

St. Thomas is a lush and beautiful island.

Sometimes her mother would take her horseback riding or swimming. Gabby recalls that Terry was an excellent swimmer, regularly swimming laps back and forth across a mile-long bay. Often, Terry would be in the water for two hours at a time, while Gabby played on the beach.

After Gabby finished seventh grade, she and Terry flew to New York to spend the summer with the Zucarellos. The first visit went so well that the two returned the following year.

After her second summer on Long Island, Gabby was ready to begin high school. Terry decided to stay in New York for a few more weeks. She sent Gabby to stay with another family friend in St. Thomas. That allowed Gabby to start ninth grade with the rest of her classmates.

By the time Terry returned to St. Thomas, Gabby had begun misbehaving. "St. Thomas is such a raw place, very destructive," Gabby described to a reporter for *USA Today*. "It's very small, so there's not a lot of room for social niceties. It was very rough and all the kids are hard."

Gabby began drinking alcohol and sneaking out at night to meet her boyfriend. She lost interest in school, and began arguing regularly with her mother. At the time, Gabby was not interested in her classes, sports, or any other productive activities.

"I started getting into trouble," Gabby admits. "I was drinking a lot, had no direction and wanted to drop out of school."

Terry had recently separated from her husband. She was worried that Gabby would get into even more trouble without a father figure to help guide her. Terry decided her daughter needed to live in a more positive environment. The two of them moved to St. Petersburg, Florida. There Terry enrolled Gabby in Keswick Christian School for her junior year.

Gabby as a senior at Keswick Christian School

Keswick is a very conservative private school that requires its students to wear uniforms and follow strict rules. After living in St. Thomas, Gabby felt like a fish out of water. Since the school is small, with only about 50 students in each grade level, everyone noticed the new tall girl on campus.

"She was taller than everyone in the school except one boy," recalls Mike Wells, Keswick's athletic director. "But Gabby handled her height well. I think she hid any insecurities she might have had."

Because of her height, the school's coaches quickly recruited her to join the girls basketball and volleyball teams. At first, Gabby had more success on the basketball court, thanks largely to her coach, Dean Soles.

The small Florida school suited Gabby very well.

Gabby describes Soles as an amazing coach with a natural gift for getting players to play well for him. Keswick's girls basketball team went to the state championships during Gabby's first season.

Gabby also enjoyed playing volleyball. "I wasn't a great [volleyball] player at first, but I had a lot of raw talent," Gabby recalls. "And I was so tall."

In her spare time, Gabby attended classes at a local modeling school. Although instructors there warned her she was too tall to be a model, Gabby quickly proved them wrong. A friend of Terry's sent photographs of Gabby to a modeling agency. Shortly afterward, an agent offered to represent her as a model. Gabby wanted to quit school and launch her professional career, but Terry said no. She realized that her daughter wasn't mature enough to begin modeling. Although Gabby was upset at the time, she later admitted that her mother had been right. "I was way too young then," she said.

By the end of her junior year, Gabby felt right at home at Keswick Christian School. She had made friends and was dating a member of the boys basketball team. On Sundays, Gabby would attend church services with her boyfriend, Jeff Sandhoff, and his family. When she and Terry left for New York for the summer, Gabby was looking forward to her senior year at Keswick.

Just before school reopened in the fall, Terry hurt her back. She decided to stay in New York to get it treated. Gabby wanted to return to Keswick School. This time, she made arrangements to live with the principal, Tim Greener, and his family until Terry was well. During the four months she lived with the Greeners, Gabby would occasionally babysit the family's two young children.

By her senior year, Gabby's volleyball game had im-_____, along with her love for the sport. ___ol's volleyball season ended, she joined ___ at competed in United States Volleyball ___rnaments. Playing in the more compet-___ helped boost her skills even more. ___de had improved immensely while she ___ick School, where she earned good ___

___ry well academically, and was popular," Mike Wells recalls. "She was independent, and seemed more mature than most of the kids."

3

A Balancing Act

During her senior year in high school, two years after she had wanted to drop out of high school, Gabby began to think seriously about attending college. Volleyball coaches at both the University of South Florida and the University of Tampa wanted Gabby to play on their team.

Gabby couldn't decide which school she liked best. Finally, in late spring, just before she graduated from Keswick Christian School, Gabby was about to make up her mind. Then, she received a third offer. Cecile Reynaud, head volleyball coach at Florida State University in Tallahassee, saw Gabby play in a tournament. Coach Reynaud was impressed with Gabby's game, and Gabby was impressed with the coach's direct manner. After visiting the FSU campus, Gabby signed a **letter of intent** to play for the Lady Seminoles.

Gabby received a $4,500 a year **athletic scholarship** to play volleyball at Florida State University. Even so, she lacked confidence in her game when she arrived on campus in the fall of 1987.

"I had no sense ever that I actually knew what I was doing," she wrote in *Big Girl in the Middle.* "If you had asked my teammates during preseason training that first year, 'Do you think Gabrielle Reece will make it?' to a one they would have said, 'No way.' "

Gabby was still on the team, and still had her scholarship, when the volleyball season started. But the tallest woman ever to play for the Seminoles watched the first six matches from the sidelines.

Gabby smacks a hit for the Seminoles.

The Seminoles needed Gabby to block and hit from her position as middle blocker.

Seven games into the season, Gabby got her first opportunity to play. She was scared. Most competitive athletes want their opponents to hit the ball at them. Gabby recalls thinking, "Please, anyone but me."

Little by little, her confidence grew. Gabby began to master the little tricks of the game and play more aggressively. The Lady Seminoles finished the 1987 season in first place in the Metro Conference with a record of 22 wins and 11 losses. After winning the postseason Metro Conference tournament, the Florida State squad competed in the NCAA tournament. The Lady Seminoles' season ended after they lost in the first round. Gabby, who tallied 175 blocks and 178 kills as a middle hitter, was voted the team's most improved player.

With her first season of college volleyball under her belt, Gabby settled in and began focusing on her classes. But soon, she had another distraction to contend with. A fashion scout had spotted Gabby walking around the campus, and encouraged her to work as a model. When the school year ended in June, Gabby flew to New York to give modeling a try. At first, she stayed at the Zucarellos' home. Then, after her former stepfather offered to cover her rent until she got established, Gabby moved into an apartment in Manhattan. After signing a contract with the IMG Models agency, Gabby earned $3,500 as a hand model for Cutex. A few weeks later, the agency made an appointment for Gabby to meet with Steven Meisel, a top fashion photographer. Meisel went wild over Gabby, and invited her to pose for Italian *Vogue* and several other international fashion magazines.

At the end of the summer, Gabby returned to the Florida State University campus. Putting her modeling career temporarily on hold, she resumed her studies and rejoined the volleyball team. Since NCAA regulations prohibit scholarship recipients from holding jobs while attending school, Gabby had to give up her athletic scholarship. Instead, she used some of her modeling earnings to pay her tuition.

For the next three years, until she graduated in the spring of 1991, Gabby would spend half a year on campus, then the remaining six months in New York.

With her height, Gabby became a dominating presence in the middle for the Florida State team.

Gabby often faced two blockers.

There, she would work as a model. She would attend the summer and fall sessions at Florida State University, then work full time between January and June. Sometimes Gabby would work on weekends in the summer, flying off to photo shoots in Europe after her last class on Friday. But once the volleyball season began, she was committed to being a full-time student-athlete.

"I would never go on a job during the season," Gabby recalled in her book. "I turned down one job, $35,000 for two days' work, because I had a game."

Despite Gabby's dedication to the volleyball team, some of her teammates were jealous. The rest of the team trained together year-round. Several players told Coach Reynaud they didn't think it was fair that Gabby was in the starting lineup after spending six months off campus. Others were upset that Gabby received so much attention.

The criticism made Gabby feel bad. But in time, she learned not to let it bother her. Like any uncomfortable situation, dealing with jealous teammates forced her to grow, she noted years later.

The Lady Seminoles won 28 games and lost just eight during Gabby's sophomore season. The Metro Conference champions won the postseason Metro Conference Tournament for the second straight year. Like the previous year, they also went to the NCAA Tournament. During their first-round match against

Colorado State, Gabby's modeling career was nearly ended when she was hit in the face with the volleyball.

Even though her nose was bleeding profusely, Gabby wasn't concerned about her looks. Instead, she was worried about her team. Would Colorado State have an advantage over the Lady Seminoles if a smaller teammate replaced Gabby? She went to the bench reluctantly, at the insistence of Coach Reynaud and the tournament officials. When the bleeding stopped, Gabby demanded to go back into the game.

"She was bound and determined that she was going to continue playing," Coach Reynaud told a reporter for a Florida State magazine. "There was not any big concern about herself. She's really a team player. That's neat for any player, no matter what her face looks like."

Despite Gabby's determination, the Lady Seminoles lost the match, which ended their season. Gabby finished the year with 350 kills and a team-leading 171 blocks. After completing her final exams, Gabby packed her bags and headed back to New York City to do more modeling.

When she switched to the Eileen Ford Agency, Gabby's modeling career really took off. She spent the summer jetting to Paris, Milan, Egypt, Rome, Mexico, the Bahamas, and the Seychelles. Gabby posed for photographers from *In Fashion*, *Vogue*, *Cosmopolitan*, *Harper's Bazaar*, and *Elle* magazines. Although she worked hard at modeling, she refused to let her success go to her head.

"It's nothing, really, if you think about it," she explained. "I mean, if you get a cover, that's great. But it's only on the stands for four weeks and then it's off the stands. I don't get too pumped up over it."

What did get Gabby pumped up was volleyball. "Athletics keep your mind clear," Gabby said in *People.* "They make your life better."

Blending athletics and modeling, Gabby kept busy throughout her college days.

During Gabby's junior season, the Lady Seminoles improved their record to 30–5. Finishing first in the Metro Conference and the postseason Metro Conference tournament, they again fell in the first round of the NCAA tourney. Gabby finished the 1989 season with 212 blocks and 333 kills, racking up numerous postseason honors. She was named to both the All-Metro and the American Volleyball Coaches All-South region teams. She also set a school record for the most solo blocks in a season with 69. Gabby received national recognition as well. In January, she was named the nation's Most Inspiring Collegiate Athlete by the Dodge National Athletic Awards Committee. *Rolling Stone* magazine also listed Gabby as one of its "Wonder Women of Sports."

During Gabby's final volleyball season at Florida State University, the Lady Seminoles dropped to third place in the Metro Conference. Florida State won 25 games but lost 10. For the third year in a row, Gabby led the team in blocking, with 189. She also had 328 kills. Her collegiate volleyball career ended after her fourth consecutive trip to the NCAA tournament. Once again, the Seminoles lost in the first round.

With her college athletic career over, Gabby again focused on being a student. In 1991, after completing all her academic requirements, she was awarded a bachelor's degree in communications. After four challenging years of balancing academics with athletics and a professional modeling career, Gabby had met her scholastic goals. The young woman who had thought she would never complete high school had a college diploma.

Can you find Gabby in this picture? She has her arm around Coach Reynaud in the back row at the right.

Gabby's beach volleyball career began in 1991.

Hitting the Beach

After graduation, Gabby moved about 500 miles southeast, from Tallahassee in the northwest end of Florida's panhandle to a coastal town near the state's southern tip. She settled in Miami, which is separated from the Atlantic Ocean by Biscayne Bay and a thin sliver of land known as Miami Beach. With her studies completed, she had more time to focus on her modeling career. There was just one problem. For four years, Gabby had been hot. But by 1991, the fashion photographers had turned to other models. Gabby had trouble finding work.

"To this day people like to say I gave up modeling for volleyball," Gabby wrote in *Big Girl in the Middle*. "In fact, people were getting tired of me. I wasn't working, and suddenly, at 21, I had no money."

Fortunately for Gabby, she had a college education and athletics to fall back on. Gabby loves playing volleyball, and she loves working out. She decided to pursue a professional volleyball career.

Teaming up with Barbara Bierman, Gabby began playing **doubles volleyball** on the beach. First Gabby and Barbara played in several practice matches against other doubles teams to get used to playing together. A few months later, they began competing in tournaments hosted by the Women's Professional Volleyball Association (WPVA). Gabby quickly realized she had a lot to learn about beach volleyball.

Gabby had spent her entire high school and college career playing a six-person game. Like other sports, such as football or soccer, six-person volleyball players specialize in either offensive or defensive positions. Different roles are assigned to different players to take advantage of their specialized abilities. In the six-person format, Gabby had specialized as a middle blocker. After years of focusing solely on blocking shots and spiking the ball, Gabby had to learn how to play doubles.

With just two players on a side, doubles players must be able to do many things. They each have to pass and be able to set the ball to their teammate. They also have to **dig,** or dive to prevent an opponent's shot from hitting the sand. Doubles players also take turns serving the ball. Many of these skills were new to Gabby. She had a difficult time adapting to the different style of play.

Gabby digs a ball hit by a beach opponent.

Gabby also had a difficult time adjusting to playing on the beach. Almost all indoor courts have wooden floors. The hard surface flexes to allow athletes to run easily and change direction quickly. Most doubles matches are played on sand courts. The soft sand gives way underneath a player's feet, slowing the player down and making it hard to move quickly.

Gabby's first tournament as a doubles player took place in Puerto Rico in early 1992. In Gabby's pro debut, she and Barbara were badly beaten, losing their match 15–4. Their second match together was even more humiliating for Gabby.

Gabby and her doubles partner talk over strategy.

A few days before the competition, *People* magazine published its annual "50 Most Beautiful People" issue. Gabby was on the list and was pictured holding a volleyball. The magazine described Gabby as a professional volleyball player, but she didn't feel like one. Gabby and Barbara were soundly defeated in the first round of the tournament. Gabby was embarrassed.

"I had no idea what I was doing," Gabby told a reporter for *Outside* magazine. "I played for half a season with the WPVA tour and got my butt kicked."

Midway through the season, Gabby decided to quit playing doubles. By that time, she was living in Southern California, where many of the doubles tournaments were held. While her original plan was to focus on her dwindling modeling career, Gabby continued to work out. Her training paid off in the spring when a new four-woman beach volleyball tour was formed. When tour organizers began drafting players for the teams, Gabby was the first woman selected.

The four-person game was much more suited to Gabby's style of play. She could play most of the game at the net as the middle blocker. In that position, Gabby's height was a huge asset. She could block shots and spike the ball.

"Four-person ball, a hybrid of indoor six-person court volleyball and doubles beach volleyball, is the perfect arena for Gabby's talents and strengths," Gabby's former college coach, Cecile Reynaud, said.

Gabby's college coach, Cecile Reynaud, encouraged Gabby to play four-person volleyball.

Gabby excelled during the league's first season, in 1992. When the season was over, Gabby was voted the MVP of the four-woman pro beach volleyball tour. Marketing executives from Lady Foot Locker invited Gabby to captain their company's team during the 1993 season. As team captain, she would select her teammates and be the team leader.

Gabby felt very comfortable on the volleyball court during her second season. Although Team Lady Foot Locker won just two tournaments in 1993, Gabby led the league in kills with 227, and in blocks, with 53. Her play attracted the attention of the marketing staff at Nike. Representatives from the athletic shoe and clothing company offered Gabby a contract. They wanted Gabby to serve as the company's first female **cross-training** representative, and appear in advertisements. The deal would allow Gabby to captain Nike's four-woman team on the pro beach volleyball tour the following season.

The offer excited Gabby. Nike would pay her a salary for training and competing. It would also provide her with free shoes and athletic wear. She knew that Nike had selected her over other volleyball players because of her modeling background.

By concentrating on improving all her skills, Gabby soon became one of the best players on the beach.

Nike hired Gabby to play volleyball and do commercials.

"When I first signed my deal, there were some people at Nike who felt that I was too feminine or too sexy to be considered an authentic athlete," Gabby told reporter Robin Roberts in a television interview on *ABC's Primetime Live*. "That's really been a fight because I think part of the reason they signed me was because of that image. Then I got there and they went, 'Now what are we going to do with this girl?' "

Gabby didn't have much time to dwell on that question. She was busy preparing for the 1994 volleyball season. As team captain, she had to evaluate players and select her teammates. She also had to work out, both in the gym, and on the volleyball court.

Nike kept Gabby busy, too, photographing her for advertisements and television commercials. She starred in a commercial called "Gabbing with Gabby," which made fun of the differences between being a model and a professional athlete. The commercial consisted of Gabby, wearing a tank top, bikini bottoms and lots of makeup, offering a series of modeling tips. Lolling on a bed, Gabby told viewers to "watch your weight, always wear smudge-proof mascara, and make the first call. Boys like it when you're aggressive." Each beauty tip was followed by an image of Gabby in action, either pumping iron, wiping the sweat off her brow during a volleyball match, or arguing a line call on the tennis court. The commercial began playing on television in September, shortly after the 1993 volleyball season ended. Gabby got a kick out of the TV ad. "I'd like people to think I have a sense of humor about myself," she told a reporter for *USA Today.*

All summer, Gabby had worked hard on her volleyball game. But when people talked about her after the commercial came out, they overlooked her volleyball skills. Instead, they talked about her TV work. After Gabby was hired as a correspondent for *MTV Sports,* she became even more well known.

Gabby's fame as a television celebrity caused some resentment among other players. Those feelings increased in April 1994, when Nike credited Gabby and designer Tinker Hatfield with having developed a new shoe called the Air Trainer Set. A couple of the players in the league were jealous that Gabby was receiving so much attention for her work off the court—as some of her college teammates had been.

"Some of the other players were a little envious and jealous," noted Gary Sato, Team Nike's coach from 1993 to 1996. "It's understandable. There are a lot of great players who've trained and played in obscurity their entire careers."

Gabby refused to let any resentments bother her. "I think the other players know where I'm at," she told reporters. "They understand my commitment to volleyball. I'm the same as them. I train. I win. I lose. I sweat. I think they're over it at this point."

5

Putting It All Together

In May 1994, Gabby began spending less time in front of the cameras and more time on the beach preparing for the upcoming tournament season. When league play began at the end of the month, she was focused solely on volleyball. Gabby didn't want any other activities to distract her from her new job as captain of Team Nike. She was also looking forward to the challenge of playing professional volleyball again. Like other top athletes, Gabby thrives on competition. She enjoys testing her skills against other top players.

Team Nike won just 3 of the 12 tournaments it entered in 1994. Gabby was disappointed with the team's record, but she was satisfied with her play. She set a league record for kills during a tournament in Chicago. There, she recorded 63 kills while attempting 173, which also set a league record for total kill attempts. When the season ended, Gabby earned individual honors. Her kill total of 454 for the season was best in the league. It was also 130 kills more than the second-place finisher. She averaged nearly 12 kills a game, with 38 percent of her kill attempts successful. Her aggressive play netted her the 1994 Offensive Player of the Year title.

Some players were jealous about the award. Gabby, who felt she had proved herself on the volleyball court, was annoyed.

"One girl made a comment to a magazine that I get so many kills only because I have more sets than anyone," she said in *Outside Kids* magazine. "C'mon, I had 150 [sic] kills more. What do I need to do?"

Gabby was too busy to dwell on jealousy. *Elle* magazine had invited her to serve as a consulting fitness editor. Nike scheduled several advertising photo sessions. Gabby also resumed her television work. She worked occasionally as a commentator on the NBA's *Inside Stuff* show. She also returned to her role as a host on *MTV Sports.* The show profiled thrill-seeking athletes in unconventional sports like sky surfing, whitewater kayaking, and road luging. She scheduled her TV shoots around her workout schedule.

Five to six mornings a week, Gabby worked out with trainer T. R. Goodman at Gold's Gym in Venice, California. Goodman designed a two-hour workout for her that included weight lifting and fitness training.

Gabby passes a ball to her setter.

The training program was grueling, and required Gabby to participate in a dozen, fast-paced exercises. Completing the workout was exhausting, she said.

"I threw up the first time I did this workout," Gabby told *Sport* magazine. "You finish and you're tired, drenched [with sweat]. Forget physical, it's mentally grinding."

Gabby spent many afternoons at the beach. There, she'd practice volleyball for several hours before heading home for dinner. Although she usually wears a two-piece outfit during matches, Gabby prefers to cover up during beach workouts. She does that to protect her skin from excessive exposure to the sun.

By working out, Gabby stays in top shape.

"I wear a hat, a T-shirt and running tights when I'm training," she notes. "I don't want a savage tan. I know what I'll look like in 10 years."

Despite her busy schedule, Gabby found time to date. Gossip columnists reported that Gabby was seen around town with actor Dean Cain, who was playing Superman on the TV show *Lois and Clark*.

When the 1995 beach volleyball season began, Gabby once again put most of her non-athletic activities on hold. And again, many people questioned how she could turn down television work for volleyball.

"This is dead serious for her," Nike coach Gary Sato explained to a reporter for the *St. Petersburg Times.* "She is committed to being the best [volleyball player] she can be. I've heard her say that her good looks she didn't earn. This takes a lot of work."

Gabby increased her kill total to 482 during the 1995 season. For the third year in a row, Gabby led the league in kills. She also repeated as the Offensive Player of the Year. Despite those personal honors, Gabby was disappointed. Team Nike won just two of the 12 tournaments it had entered. Gabby wished the team had done better, but she didn't have much time to worry about the past.

After the season ended, Gabby concentrated on a new job. She began working as the host of a TV show called *The Extremists.* Like *MTV Sports*, her new show focused on high-action sports. Gabby participated in many of the sports activities, like water skiing and boxing. The show was syndicated and broadcast in 40 countries.

The work was fast-paced. One week, Gabby filmed seven new segments. Often, she would travel with a film crew to profile extreme-sport athletes. One day, the job took her to the Hawaiian island of Maui to film daredevil surfers. There, she met Laird Hamilton, who rides some of the world's biggest waves. They began spending a lot of time together. When the 1996 beach volleyball season began, Laird traveled with Gabby to all her tournaments.

Gabby had a lot of company on the road that season. Her manager, Jane Kachmer, went to many of her games. So did writer Karen Karbo, who was working on a book with Gabby. Published in 1997, the book told the story of a year in the life of former super model turned volleyball player. It included brief portions written by Gabby.

The 1996 season was a difficult one for Gabby. Team Nike won just 1 of the 10 tournaments it competed in. As team captain, Gabby made numerous roster changes in an effort to find a winning combination of players. In July, midway through the season, she fired coach Gary Sato. She replaced Sato, who had been with the team for more than three years, with coach Charlie Brand.

Gabby was relieved when the season finally ended.

Teamwork is an important part of beach ball.

Even setting another league record for kills—547—
didn't make her feel better.

"I was discouraged," she admitted. "But I still think
I had a decent perspective. I knew I'd be able to get
revved up again."

She took a vacation before starting her off-season
workouts. *The Extremists* had been canceled, so
Gabby spent less time in front of the camera following the 1996 season. She appeared on a few talk
shows and had a walk-on role in a television sitcom.

Gabby's long arms give her an advantage at the net.

She also spent some time writing a fitness column for *Sports for Women* magazine.

During the offseason, the organizers of the beach volleyball tour made an important change. Instead of allowing team captains to draft players, the tour director would select the teams for the 1997 season. Setter Stephanie Cox and hitters Katy Eldridge and Jenny Johnson joined Gabby on Team Nike. It proved to be a winning combination. After coming in second and third during the first two competitions, Team Nike won four straight tournaments.

"My season, overall, is going well," Gabby told a reporter for *The Oregonian* in late July. While losing had made matches seem like a chore during previous seasons, winning made competing a pleasant task. "Volleyball's a lot of fun [right now]," Gabby said.

Although the team was unable to sustain its winning ways, Nike finished the 12-tournament season in second place. Team Paul Mitchell barely squeaked past Nike to capture first place for the 1997 season.

Gabby finished the season in third place on the kills list, with 321. Diane Shoemaker, Team Paul Mitchell's middle blocker, finished first with 354. Outside hitter Annett Davis, was second with 336.

Although Gabby's four-year reign as the league's kill leader ended, she received other honors that summer. *Women's Sports and Fitness* published an article on "The 20 Most Influential Women in Sports."

Gabby, whose picture appeared on the magazine's cover, was included in that list of athletes. Gabby told readers her success came from her commitment to being the best in her sport, and hard work.

"Young girls have this perception of me that it's all very easy," she said in the article. "But if there's going to be any glamour, it's usually the result of mundane fundamentals."

By "mundane fundamentals," Gabby means spending hours working out in the gym and on the volleyball court. She trains regularly, even on days when she'd rather be relaxing with friends. Her dedication has helped her achieve success both on and off the volleyball court.

The pro beach volleyball tour took the summer of 1998 off but Gabby kept working on her skills.

Career Highlights

Florida State University

Year	Kills	Blocks
1987	178	175
1988	350	171
1989	333	212
1990	328	189
Totals	1,189	747

- Fifth on the NCAA career blocks list
- All-Metro teams, 1989, 1990
- American Volleyball Coaches All-South region teams, 1989, 1990
- Florida State record, solo blocks in a season, 1989

Pro Beach Volleyball

Year	Team	Victories
1993	Lady Foot Locker	2
1994	Nike	3
1995	Nike	2
1996	Nike	0
1997	Nike	4, co-champions

- Pro Beach Volleyball kill leader, 1994, 1995, 1996
- Pro Beach Volleyball Offensive Player of the Year, 1994, 1995
- Pro Beach Volleyball kills/blocks leader, 1993

Glossary

athletic scholarship: Money a college or organization gives a student-athlete to pay for his or her education. Colleges often award scholarships to students who are outstanding athletes, scholars, musicians, or leaders.

cross-training: Using a variety of sports to become physically fit. Athletes often choose to run some days, bike others, and lift weights on other days. In this way, most of the muscles in the athlete's body are exercised but not in exactly the same way. This helps prevent over-use injuries.

dig: A return or pass of a hard-hit ball.

doubles volleyball: A variation of volleyball in which there are just two players on a team. The two must cover the entire court, using all the skills.

kill: Hitting the ball so that it lands on the opponent's side of the court, scoring a point or sideout for the hitting team.

letter of intent: A letter in which a high school student-athlete says which college he or she plans to attend.

middle blocker: The player whose job it is to block hitting attempts by the other team. A middle blocker usually plays by the middle of the net. A middle blocker is also called a middle hitter.

Gabby hits against a strong middle blocker.

outside hitter: The player whose job it is to hit from one end of the net.

round-robin tournament: A tournament in which a team plays every other team.

setter: The player whose job it is to put the ball in position for a player to spike.

Sources

Information for this book was obtained from the following sources: Jack Beamish *(Florida State,* Fall 1989); CE Sports Bud Light Pro Beach Volleyball Tour media guide and press releases; Bill Coats *(St. Louis Post-Dispatch,* 30 June 1996); Mark Conley *(Santa Cruz Sentinel,* 31 August 1996); John Cotey *(St. Petersburg Times,* 24 May 1996); Dan Dieffenbach *(Sport,* April 1995); Florida State University Sports Information Department media guide and player statistics; Karen Karbo *(Outside,* October 1995); Katy Muldoon *(Oregonian,* 7 August 1997); Gabrielle Reece and Karen Karbo *(Big Girl in the Middle,* Crown, 1997); Susan Reed *(People Weekly,* 16 October 1989); Jim Servin *(Harper's Bazaar,* June 1994); Michael Silver *(Sports Illustrated,* special issue, Winter 1997); Jim Spadafore *(The Detroit News,* 13 June 1996); Rob Story *(Outside Kids,* Summer 1995); Susan Swimmer *(Seventeen,* May 1994); Karen Thomas *(USA Today,* 2 August 1993); *Volleyball,* August 1997, September 1997; Jean Weiss *(Women's Sports and Fitness,* July/August 1997); and the author's telephone interview with Mike Wells.

Index

Write to Gabby

You can send mail to Gabby at the address on the right. If you write a letter, don't get your hopes up too high. Gabby and other athletes get lots of letters every day, and they aren't always able to answer them all.

Gabrielle Reece
c/o Jane Kachmer Management
5111 Ocean Front Walk #4
Marina Del Rey CA 90202

Acknowledgments

Photographs reproduced with permission of:
© Agostini/Gamma Liason, p. 1; © ALLSPORT USA/Markus Boesch, pp. 2, 6, 11, 39, 44, 47, 48, 56, 58; © ALLSPORT USA/Tony Duffy, p. 8; © Spooner/Gamma Liason, p. 9; Seth Poppel Yearbook Archives, pp. 14, 21, 22; Courtesy of Gabrielle Reece, pp. 16, 18; © W. Lynn Seldon Jr., p. 19; © ALLSPORT USA/Tim DeFrisco, pp. 24, 29; Courtesy of Florida State University/Department of Athletics, pp. 26, 27, 30, 35, 42; © Exley/Gamma Liason, p. 33; Photo by John English, pp. 36, 40, 43; Sportschrome East/West, pp. 51, 55, 61; © ALLSPORT USA/ Mike Hewitt, p. 54;

Front cover photograph by © ALLSPORT USA/Markus Boesch.
Back cover photograph by © ALLSPORT USA/Tony Duffy.
Artwork by Michael Tacheny.

About the Author

Terri Morgan is a freelance writer and sports fan from Soquel, California. Her articles have appeared in more than four dozen magazines and newspapers. Her other books for Lerner include *Photography: Take Your Best Shot, Chris Mullin, Steve Young* (all with Shmuel Thaler), *Ruthie Bolton-Holifield,* and *Junior Seau.* When not writing, Terri enjoys surfing, walking her dogs, playing baseball, and watching sports.